Soil-Our Life Support System

Om KIDZ
An imprint of Om Books International

Little Ron was very excited. His family had shifted to a new house. He ran to the backyard with Buddy, his soft, white puppy. “Yippie! there are so many trees, vegetables and flowers growing here!” he exclaimed.

“It is because the soil in this area is very fertile,” his Dad told him.

“What is soil, Dad? Ron asked, confused.

Dad picked up a bit of mud from near a tree and showed it to Ron.

"This is soil. Like air and water, this too is a natural resource. There wouldn't be any life on earth without it. You will be surprised to know that it takes thousands of years for this much of soil to form from decayed animals and dissolved bits of rocks and minerals," Dad explained.

Buddy was having fun rolling in the mud. "Buddy, it is dirty!"Ron scolded his puppy.

Mom was plucking some vegetables for dinner. She said, "No, Ron. This mud is not all dirt. You get to eat these fruits and vegetables because this mud or soil contains the nutrients that help them to grow."

Ron suddenly noticed an earthworm wriggling in the soil. “What’s that, Mom?” he shrieked.

Mom laughed. “Soil is not only something on which we walk, build and grow trees and plants. Many living things like earthworms, ants, insects and bacteria also live in it. In return, these creatures help in making the soil fertile,” she said.

Dad came out with a china bowl filled with milk for the puppy. "Guess what this bowl is made of !" he said to Ron. Seeing his puzzled look, Dad chuckled. "This is made of clay, which is also a type of soil. Even the bricks used for constructing this house are made from clay."Ron had never thought that soil was so important in our lives. He now wanted to help in making the soil of his backyard even more fertile.

Ron picked up the hose pipe and started watering the plants. Mom gently told him that he is harming the plants with too much watering. Now Ron was confused.

"Let's make a mud hill," Mom suggested. So all three set about to make a pretty little hill of mud. Ron placed plastic people, cardboard houses, trees and toy cars. He was very happy. Then mom sprayed water on it with a hose. Ron saw the people, houses, cars and trees slide down the mound. "This is soil erosion," Mom softly told him.

Ron now understood that plants loosen their hold on soil with too much water or rainfall. Soil binds the plants which in turn bind the soil. He wanted to know more about soil erosion."Erosion takes place even in areas where there is no rain. The wind blows away the dry soil,"Dad added.

"Overgrazing by animals, cutting down trees for cooking and other purposes also erodes the soil." Mom said.

By now, Ron was fascinated by the subject of soil to which he had never given any importance earlier. He imagined a real hillside with trees. "What can be done to slow down or stop the soil on the hillside from eroding?" he wondered aloud.

"Mainly by planting more trees and rocks on the slope," Mom had a ready answer.

Next morning, Ron had a bright idea. “Dad, can we plant a date palm and a coconut tree here? It would be so much fun!” he said, his face shining with excitement.

“Ron, every plant needs a different type of soil to grow. This soil is not suitable for coconuts and date palms,” Dad told his disappointed son.

“There are various types of soils,” he continued.

"There is sandy soil, silt soil, clay soil and loamy soil, each of which has a different characteristic to help a particular variety of plant to grow."

One day, dad was digging a compost pit to make fertiliser. Ron saw that the colour of the soil had become lighter beneath. Dad explained, "Soil has four layers.The upper layer covering the earth's surface is called Humus. The layer below this is the Topsoil which contains minerals and roots of plants. If you dig deeper, you will find the Subsoil which is mostly rock. The roots of big trees reach till down there. The Bedrock is the deepest layer which is solid rock."

Mom then brought the leftover food, skin of peeled vegetables and fruits from the house and threw them in the compost pit. "We are making organic fertilisers to make our soil even more fertile," she told Ron. From then on, Ron was careful to throw every such compost material into the pit.

It was 5th December. Ron was watching the TV. The Food and Agriculture Organisation of the United Nations was celebrating 'World Soil Day' to create awareness about soil pollution. Ron nodded. By now, he already knew that soil is our life support system and needs to be protected.